AF270591

NFL Teams

HOUSTON
TEXANS
TEXANS
KENNY ABDO
Fly!
An Imprint of Abdo Zoom
abdobooks.com

abdobooks.com

Published by Abdo Zoom, a division of ABDO, P.O. Box 398166, Minneapolis, Minnesota 55439. Copyright © 2022 by Abdo Consulting Group, Inc. International copyrights reserved in all countries. No part of this book may be reproduced in any form without written permission from the publisher. Fly!™ is a trademark and logo of Abdo Zoom.

Printed in China.
052021
092021

Photo Credits: AP Images, Icon Sportswire, iStock, Shutterstock PREMIER
Production Contributors: Kenny Abdo, Jennie Forsberg, Grace Hansen
Design Contributors: Candice Keimig, Neil Klinepier

Library of Congress Control Number: 2020919498

Publisher's Cataloging-in-Publication Data

Names: Abdo, Kenny, author.
Title: Houston Texans / by Kenny Abdo
Description: Minneapolis, Minnesota : Abdo Zoom, 2022 | Series: NFL teams |
    Includes online resources and index.
Identifiers: ISBN 9781098224639 (lib. bdg.) | ISBN 9781098225575 (ebook) |
    ISBN 9781098226046 (Read-to-Me ebook)
Subjects: LCSH: Houston Texans (Football team)--Juvenile literature. | National
    Football League--Juvenile literature. | Football teams--Juvenile literature. |
    American football--Juvenile literature. | Professional sports--Juvenile literature.
Classification: DDC 796.33264--dc23

TABLE OF CONTENTS

HOUSTON TEXANS

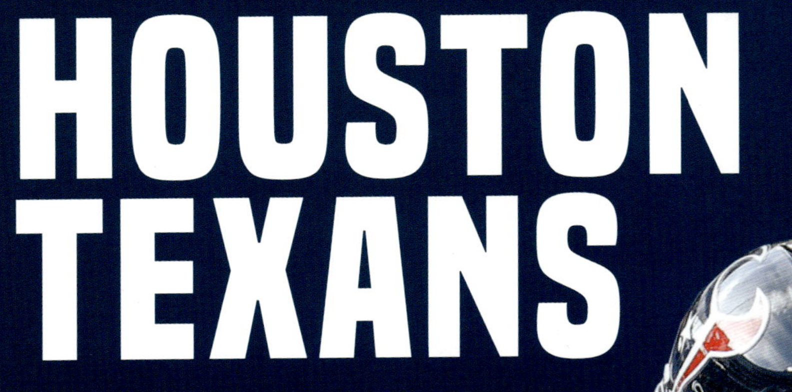

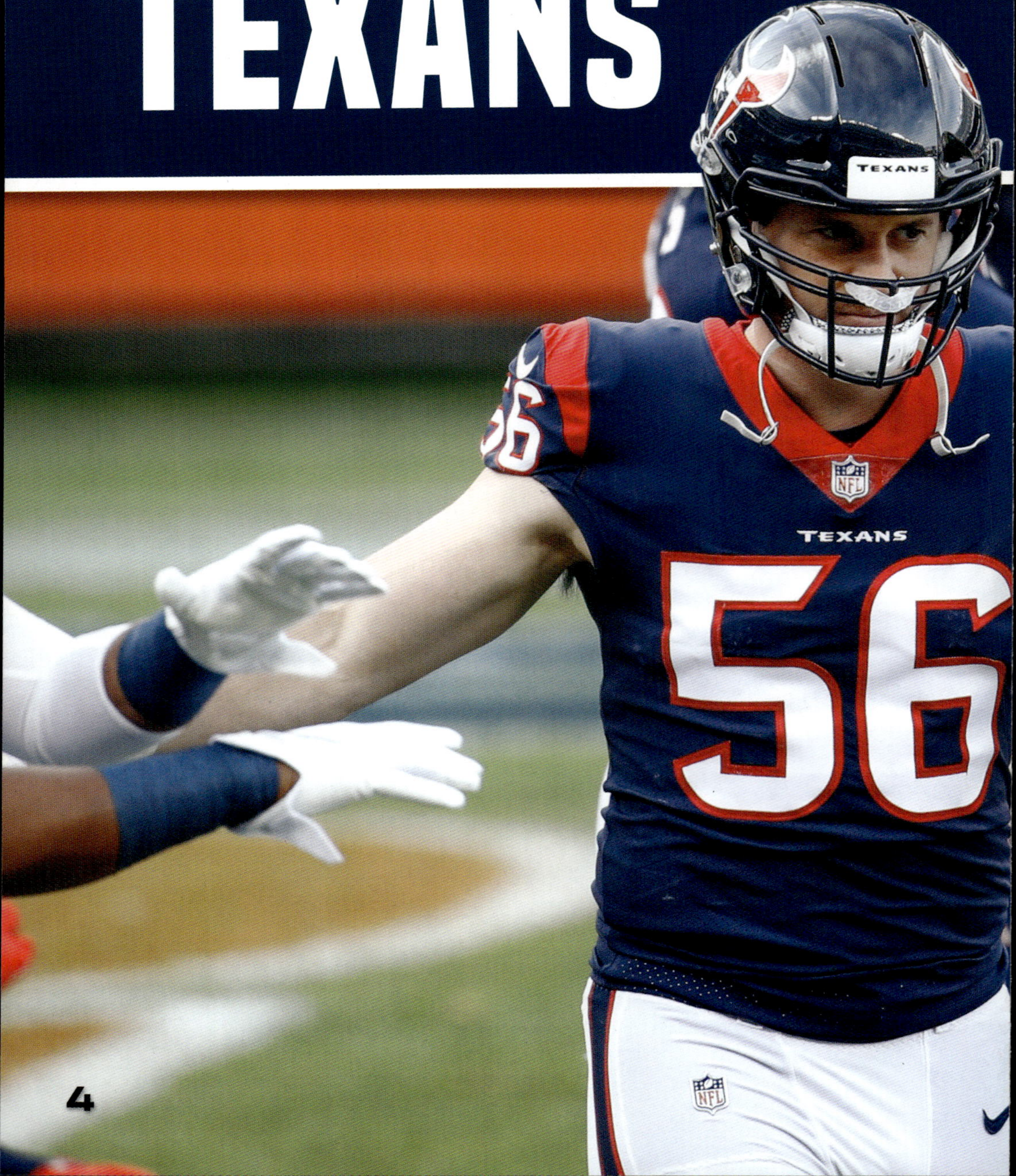

Rocking the red, white, and blue uniforms, the Houston Texans have more than just a lone star on the roster.

With visits to the playoffs and several division titles, the Texans are one of four NFL teams to never make it to the **Super Bowl**.

KICK OFF

Houstonians rejoiced when businessman Robert McNair brought pro football back to the Texas city in 1999. The Oilers had left for Nashville just a few years prior.

The Texans played their first game at home to a sellout crowd on September 8, 2002. Beating the Dallas Cowboys, it was the first time that a new team won its debut NFL game since 1961.

TEXANS
31
C.SMITH
22
Riddell
Wilson

The excitement from the team's first game did not translate into lots of future victories. The Texans had their worst season in 2005, winning only two games. They would repeat that losing 2-14 record again eight seasons later.

TEAM RECAPS

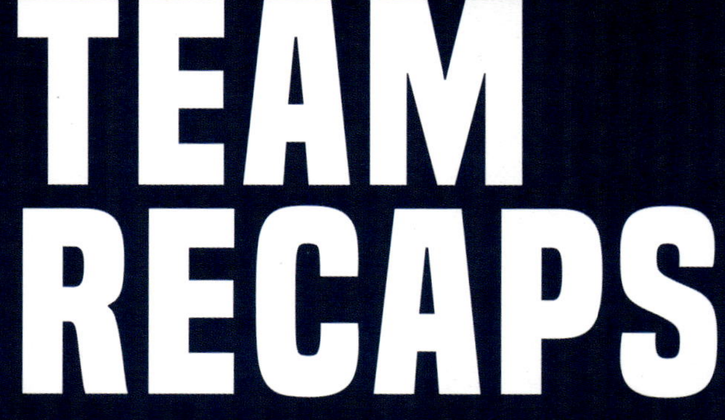

The Texans had their first winning season in 2009! **Quarterback** Matt Schaub led the **league** in passing yards.

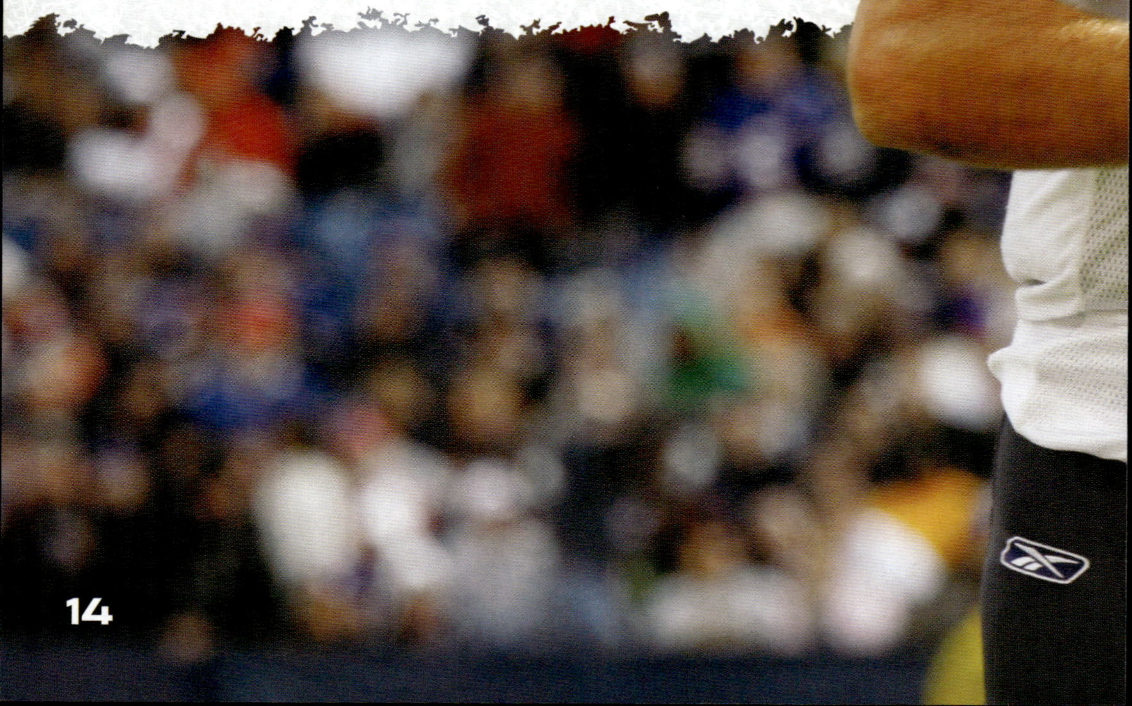

The Texans finished the regular 2012 season with a 12–4 record, the best in team history!

JOHNSON
13

Between 2011 and 2019, the Texans won the **AFC** South Division title an incredible six times!

The Texans finished the 2019 season with a 10-6 record. They beat the Bills in the **Wild Card** Playoff game. Deshaun Watson, DeAndre Hopkins, and Laremy Tunsil were all chosen for the **Pro Bowl**!

21

The 2020 season began with a 0–4 start. The Texans let general manager and coach Bill O'Brien go. Associate coach Romeo Crennel replaced O'Brien as head coach, before David Culley stepped into the position.

GRIFFIN
84
88
17

Andre Johnson became a Texan in 2003. He set a lot of records, despite many injuries. Johnson became the first Texans player to reach 10,000 receiving yards in 2012! He also set a team record for most career receptions.

TEXANS
80

Arian Foster joined the Texans in 2009. He holds the records for total rushing yards and rushing touchdowns for the team. He led the NFL in rushing touchdowns in 2010 and 2012. Foster played in four **Pro Bowls** from 2010 to 2014.

DeAndre Hopkins was drafted in the first round by the Texans in 2013. He had his first 100-yard receiving game in the second game of his **rookie** season. In 2015, Hopkins broke the team's record for most touchdown receptions in one season.

GLOSSARY

American Football Conference (AFC) – one of two major conferences of the NFL. Each conference contains 16 teams split into four divisions. The winner of the AFC championship plays the NFC winner at the Super Bowl.

league – a group of teams that compete against each other.

Pro Bowl – a game played once a year between two teams comprised of the NFL's all-stars.

quarterback (QB) – the player on the offensive team that directs teammates in their play.

rookie – a first-year player in a professional sport.

Super Bowl – the NFL championship game, played once a year.

Wild Card Round – the first round of the playoffs. Each of the two conferences send four division champions and three wild-card teams to its postseason.

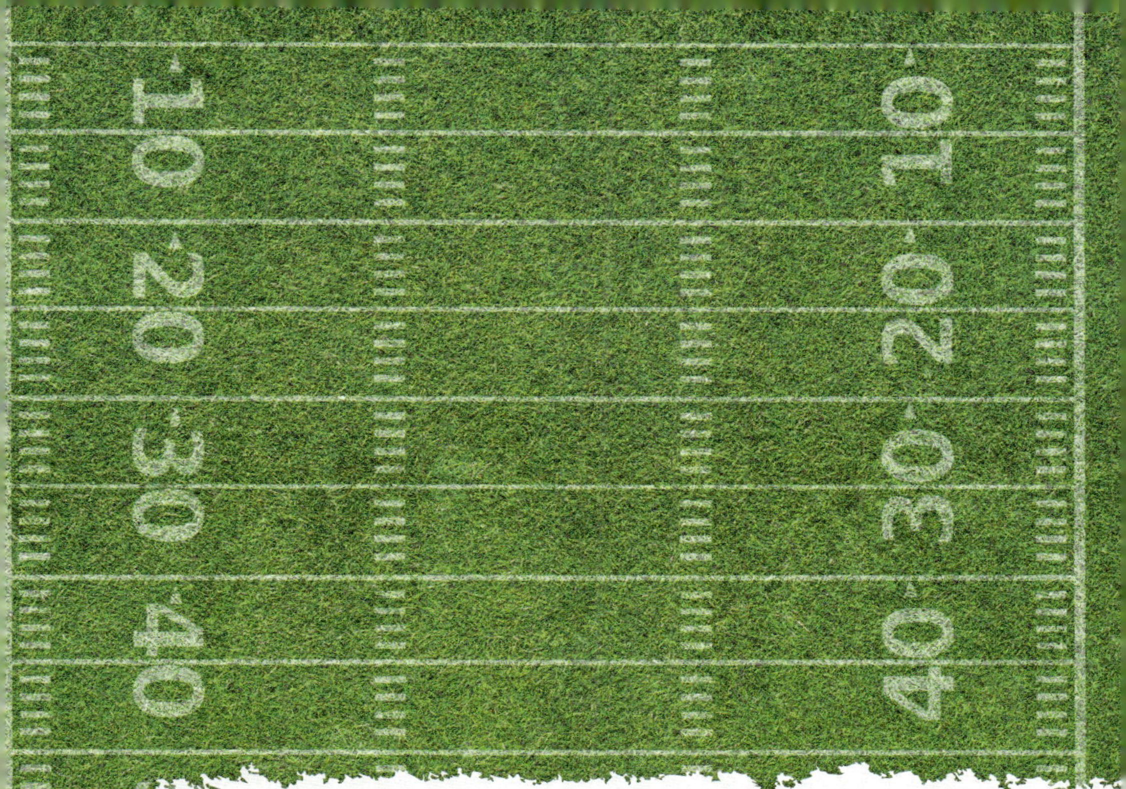

ONLINE RESOURCES

To learn more about the Houston Texans, please visit **abdobooklinks.com** or scan this QR code. These links are routinely monitored and updated to provide the most current information available.

INDEX